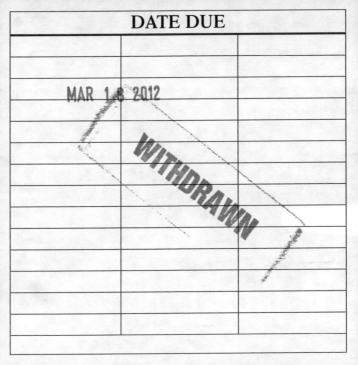

THE
BIG BOOK
OF
REAL TRAINS

TEXT BY ELIZABETH CAMERON

ILLUSTRATED BY GEORGE J. ZAFFO

GROSSET & DUNLAP • PUBLISHERS • NEW YORK

ISBN: 0-448-02140-4 (Trade Edition)
ISBN: 0-448-03685-1 (Library Edition)
© 1949, 1953, 1963, by Grosset & Dunlap, Inc.

1975 PRINTING

THE LOCOMOTIVE AND TENDER · The engine comes out of the roundhouse. It is cleaned and oiled. The tender behind the engine carries coal and water. The locomotive is ready for a trip. This locomotive has four pilot

wheels in front. These keep the engine on a track. It has six driving wheels.
These make the engine go. Four other wheels carry the back of the engine.

HOPPER · A steel hopper car carries coal and gravel. It also carries different kinds of ore. A hopper is loaded from the top. It is loaded by an auto-

matic loader. A switch engine moves the hopper under the loading bin. The coal or gravel goes through the chutes into the hopper.

NYC
8 801 00
CAPY. 140 000
LD. LML 156 000
LT. WT. 54 000

COVERED HOPPER · The covered hopper has a roof over the top. There are eight hatches on the roof. The hatches are opened to load the

hopper. The covered hopper carries sugar, cement or grain. No moisture can get in to harden the hopper's cargo.

FLAT CAR · A flat car is a platform on wheels. It has no top or walls. It has stakes instead along the sides. The stakes keep the cargo in the flat car from falling off. Flat cars can haul large pieces of machinery. They also haul

huge logs and boards from the sawmills. Sometimes big tractors are carried on a flat car.

SUPER FLAT CAR · The super flat car has thirty-two wheels. The center of the super flat car is depressed. Huge heavy machinery or electric

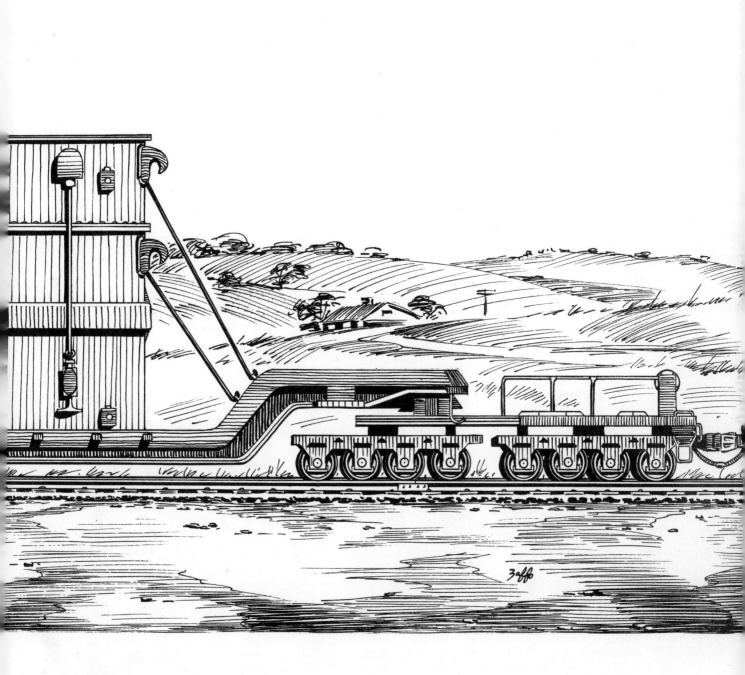

transformers are carried in the depressed center. The center is depressed so that the car can go under bridges with its cargo.

CATTLE CAR · This livestock car carries cattle. It has one deck. It has slits on each side to let in fresh air for the animals. Some livestock cars carry sheep and pigs. They have two decks. Cars that carry chickens and turkeys have

many decks. Animals cannot travel more than a day and a half in a freight car. This is the law. The cattle cars stop at resting places. The animals have food and water in the resting pens. They have time to exercise, too.

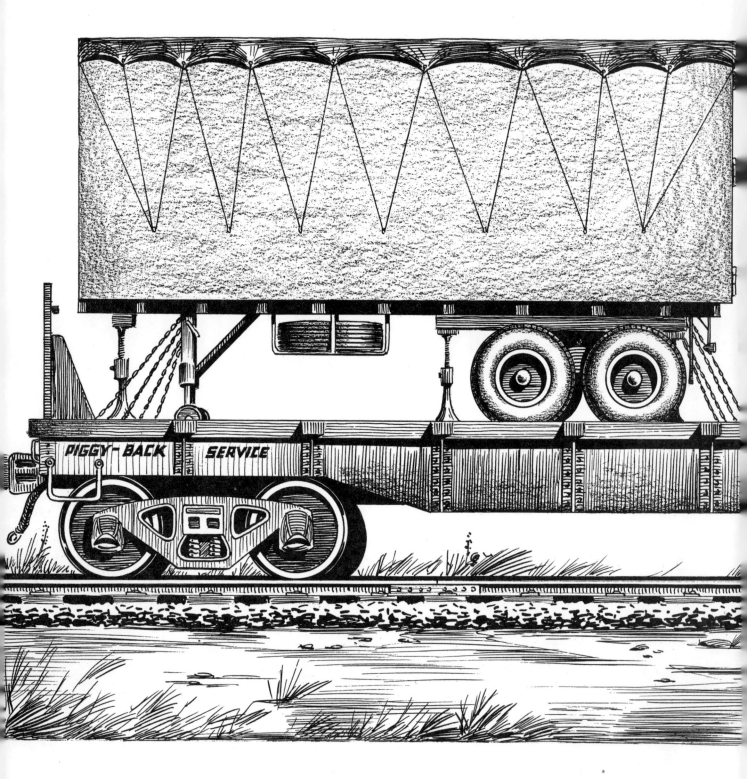

PIGGY-BACK CAR · The piggy-back car carries trailer boxes. Some piggy-back cars carry one trailer box. Others carry two. Some trains are made up only of piggy-back cars. These trains travel mostly at night. The

trailer box is secured to the deck of the piggy-back car. Jacks are placed
under the box. The jacks hold the body of the trailer box up, in case the
box gets a flat tire.

THE GONDOLA · The gondola is a metal box on wheels. It has no top. It carries things that snow and rain cannot hurt. It is loaded and unloaded by men. Sometimes the men use machines to load the car.

Gondolas haul pieces of machinery. They haul pipes, cement blocks, steel plates and other things.

AUTO CAR · The auto car carries new cars from the factory. It carries them to all parts of the country. Each auto car carries nine standard-size

cars. The auto car can carry fifteen compact cars. Automobiles ride safely in the auto car.

THE REFRIGERATOR CAR • A refrigerator car carries fruits and vegetables. It carries meat and fish. It carries butter and eggs. It even carries fresh flowers.

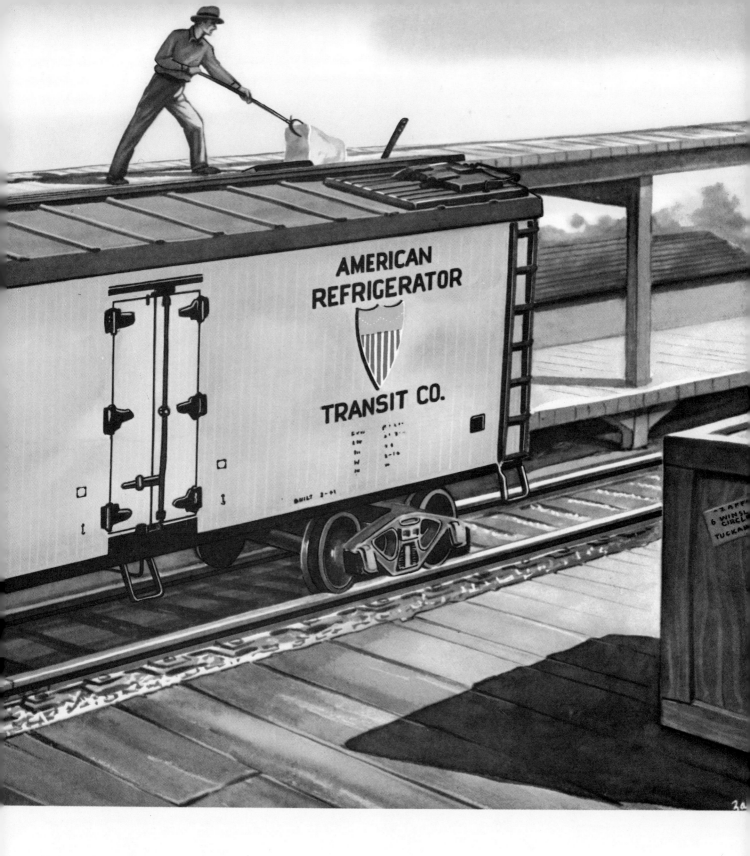

Men fit canvas funnels over the doors. Machines blow cold air into the car.
Then the car is loaded. The doors are closed. Ice is put in at each end of the
refrigerator car. More ice is put in at stations along the way.

MECHANICAL TEMPERATURE CONTROLLED CAR

Santa Fe

SFRD

2213

CAPY. 124 000 RP
LD. LMT. 124 000
LT. WT. 86 000

DIESEL FUEL Nº 1

MECHANICAL REFRIGERATOR CAR · The mechanical refrigerator car carries its own refrigerator. The refrigerator is run by diesel fuel. The temperature in the car can be kept at 70°, or as low as 10° below

zero. A mechanical refrigerator car carries fresh fruits and vegetables. It
can also carry frozen foods.

TANK CAR • Tank cars are really big cans with different kinds of linings. Milk tank cars have glass or steel linings. Cars that carry chemicals are lined with rubber, lead or aluminum. Tank cars have one or more

domes on top. In warm weather the liquid expands and goes up in the dome. If the liquid could not expand, the car might break at the seams. There are more than 200 different kinds of tank cars.

DOUBLE-DOOR BOX CAR · The double-door on the box car makes it easy to load and unload large cargo. The box car carries dry goods that are packed in boxes. It carries barrels and bales. It carries bundles and bags.

ROUTE OF THE
VISTA-DOME
NORTH COAST
LIMITED

NORTHERN PACIFIC
RAILWAY

EXW 10-7
EW 9-5
IL 40-6
IW 9-2
IH 10-6
CU.FT. 3727

It even carries small boats. The box car is made of metal in the outside and lined with wood on the inside.

CABOOSE · The caboose is the last car of the train. It is an office, a bedroom, and a kitchen. The rear brakeman sits in the place on top and watches the whole train. On long trips the train crew cooks dinner in the caboose.

The caboose has a telephone. The crew can talk to the engineer and the fire-man up front.

CLASSIFICATION YARD · The classification yard is where you can see all kinds of freight cars. New trains are made up at one end of the yard. Incoming trains are "cut" at the classification yard. Cars that are to remain at this yard for unloading or loading are put on certain tracks. Cars that are to go on to the next terminal are put on other tracks. The train that is

being cut is at the highest point of the yard. This is called the "hump." As each car (or group of cars) is cut, it coasts downhill. Men in the two towers control the retarders. These retarders act as brakes on the coasting cars. The cars are made to slow up just enough so that they won't bang into the parked cars on the track that they are approaching.

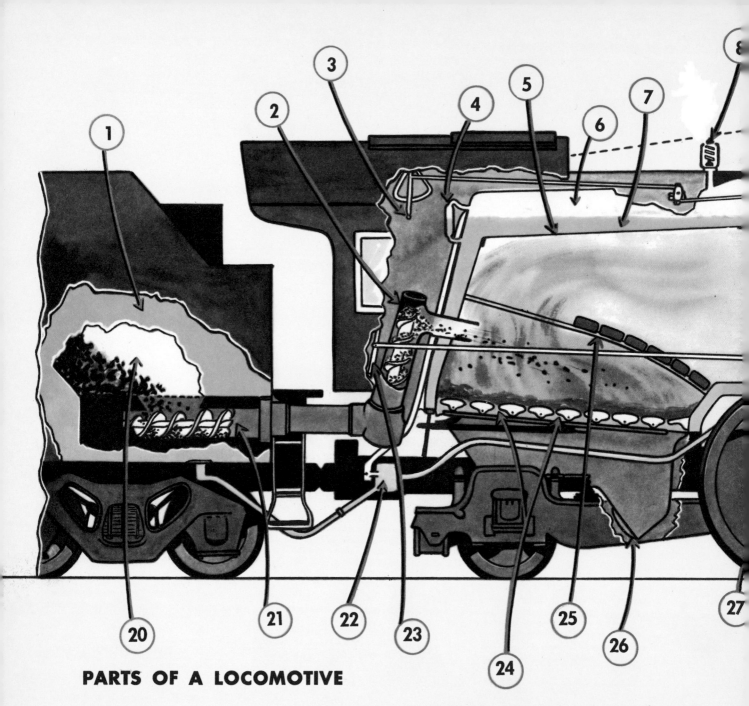

PARTS OF A LOCOMOTIVE

1 Water Tank.

2 Stoker. Coal is carried to the stoker. Steam jets blow it to all parts of the fire bed.

3 Throttle Lever.

4 Water Gauge. It shows how much water is in the boiler. Water must always cover the crown sheet. (See 5.)

5 Crown Sheet. Moist steam is blown over the crown sheet. This is the hottest part of the firebox.

6 Steam.

7 Water.

8 Safety Valve. It opens to keep the steam pressure from getting too high.

9 Throttle Valve. It controls steam that runs the locomotive.

10 Dry Pipe. It carries steam to the valve and cylinders. (See 18 and 19.)

11 Bell. It rings by air pressure.

12 Water Delivery Pipe. (See 22.)

13 Sand Dome. Sand is blown down the sand pipes if the track is slippery. (See 14.)

14 Sand Pipe.

15 Superheater Tubes.

16 Smokebox. It is filled with exhaust gases.

17 Valve Piston. It guides steam in and out of the cylinder.

18 Valve.

19 Cylinder.

20 Coal Bunker.

21 Worm Coal Conveyer.

22 Injector. Water comes from the tender to
the injector. It mixes with a jet of steam.
The steam and water push their way up
the delivery pipe and into the boiler.

23 Reverse Lever.

24 Grate.

25 Brick Arch.

26 Ashpan Hopper. It lets out ashes from the
grate. (See 24.)

27 Eccentric Crank.

28 Eccentric Rod.

29 Main Rod. It gets its power from the
piston. (See 35.)

30 Side Rod. It takes power from the main
rod to both large wheels.

31 Radius Rod. It controls the engine going
forward and going backward. The radius
rod is lifted up when the engine goes the
other way.

32 Valve Gear. It controls the going-up or
going-down of the radius rod.

33 Sand Pipe Outlet.

34 Crosshead. It is the place where the main
rod joins the piston.

35 Piston. Steam comes in from the right
through the dry pipe and pushes the piston
to the left. This pushes the main rod and
makes the engine go.

DIESEL SWITCHER · The diesel switch engine is the work horse of the yard. It is used to push or pull the many freight cars in the yard. The switch engine is used to make up a new train. It is used to move new cars to different sidings in the yard.

This diesel switch engine has the power to pull about forty-five freight cars. Railroad men call the switch engine a "drill" engine.

TRAIN

WHISTLE SIGNALS

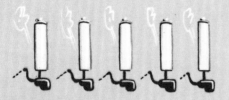

A SERIES OF SHORT TOOTS
Alarm for persons or
animals on track.

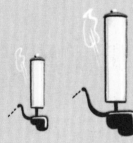

3 SHORT TOOTS
A. Back up (when train is still).
B. Stop at next station (when running).

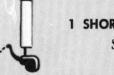

1 SHORT TOOT
Stop.

1 SHORT — 1 LONG TOOT
Brakes sticking, or inspect
train line for leak

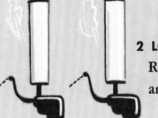

2 LONG TOOTS
Release brakes
and go ahead.

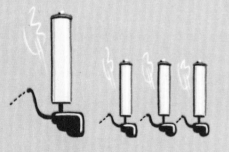

1 LONG — 3 SHORT TOOTS
Flagman, guard
rear of train.

1 LONG TOOT
Approaching station,
rail crossing, or tunnel.

AIR SIGNAL CORD

2 PULLS ON CORD
A. Start (when train is still).
B. Stop at once (when running).

3 PULLS ON CORD
A. Back train (when still).
B. Stop at next passenger station
(when running).

SIGNALS

LANTERN SIGNALS

STOP

Swing back and
forth across track

REDUCE SPEED

Held at arm's length

PROCEED

Raised and lowered

TRAIN PARTED

Swing in circle at arm's
length across tracks

APPLY AIR BRAKES

Swing above head

RELEASE AIR BRAKES

Held at arm's length
above the head

EMERGENCY STOP SIGNALS

This is Unit "A" of a two-unit locomotive. Unit "A" contains the cab where the engineer and the fireman sit

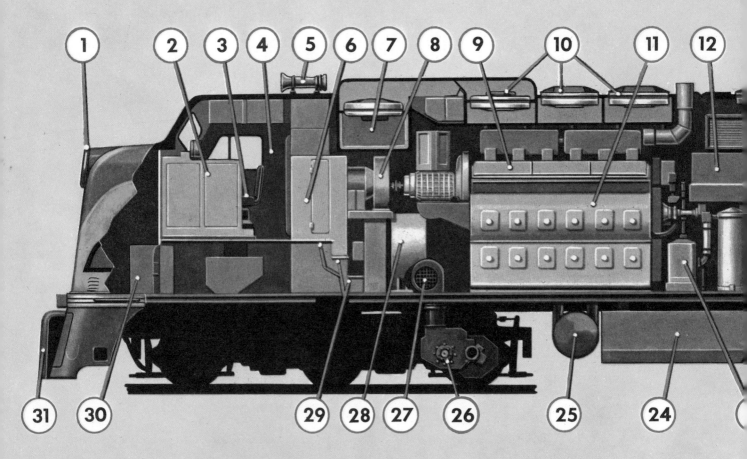

KEY TO NUMBERS

1. Headlight
2. Control Unit
3. Engineer's Seat
4. Cab
5. Horn
6. Electrical Cabinets
7. Ventilation Hatch
8. Traction Motor Blower
9. Fuel Injectors

10. Cooling System (A.C. Motor-Driven Fans)
11. 12-Cylinder Diesel Engine (1125 h.p.). There are two engines in this unit, making a total of 2250 h.p.
12. Oil Cooler
13. Dynamic Brakes
14. Outer Shell of Locomotive. The other 1125-h.p. engine is inside.

15. Separate Steam Generator Room	24. Combination Fuel and Water Tank
16. Coupler	1200 gals. of fuel, 1350 gals. of water
17. Toilet	25. Main Air Reservoirs
18. Brake Cylinder	26. Traction Motor
19. Springs	27. Blower, for Traction Motor
20. Brake Shoes	28. Main Generator
21. Sand Pipe	29. Steps
22. Main Air Reservoirs	30. Air-Brake Equipment
23. Water-Cooled Air Compressor	31. Pilot

THE MEN WHO RUN THE TRAINS

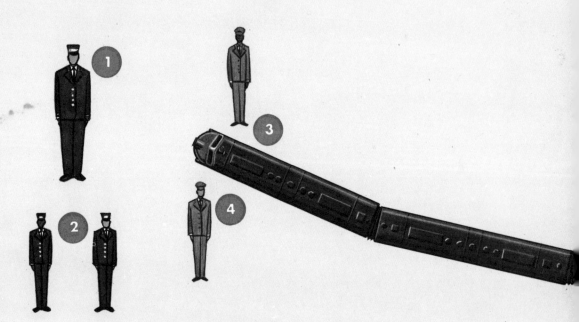

1. *Conductor:* Captain of the train, his word is law. He watches over the welfare of the passengers and crew.
2. *Trainmen:* Two men who help collect tickets and aid conductor in safe operation of the train.
3. *Engineer:* Head man in the cab, who runs the locomotive and is responsible for its speeds, signals and safety.
4. *Fireman:* Second man in the cab, who helps the engineer check the road signals and other safety measures.
5. *Pullman Conductors:* Two "lieutenants" under the conductor, who collect reservations for Pullman space.
6. *Porter:* Every sleeping car and Pullman chair car has a porter who helps to make the passengers comfortable.

A crew of 38 men is required to perform the many services for safe, comfortable and convenient travel aboard a streamliner like the Pennsylvania Railroad's Congressional Limited. This drawing shows where each man is assigned.

7. *Stewards*: Two men in charge of dining and kitchen cars. They order supplies and provide for seating and comfort of guests.

8. *Chef*: Top man in the kitchen, he has charge of the proper preparation of the food.

9. *Cooks*: Three men who assist the chef in preparing the meals and menus of the day.

10. *Pantryman*: The "middle-man" between the kitchen crew and the waiters. He watches over the niceties of customer service.

11. *Waiters*: Eight men who serve the guests.

A. *Kitchen-Lounge*: Half of the car is the kitchen where all the food is prepared. The other half is a lounge where beverages are served.

B. *Full-Length Diner*: The restaurant on the train.